I0462593

Tribal Designs Coloring Book

Animals ~ Snakes ~ Flowers
Coloring Book

_____

Sandra Bacon

Tribal Designs Coloring Book
Copyright © 2019 By Sandra Bacon

All rights are reserved. No part of this publication may be reproduced, stored in a retrieval system or transmitten in any way or by any means. This means electronic, mechanical, photocopying, recording or otherwise, without the prior written consent of the author of this publication. Any person or persons who do may be liable to criminal prosecution and civil claims for damages.

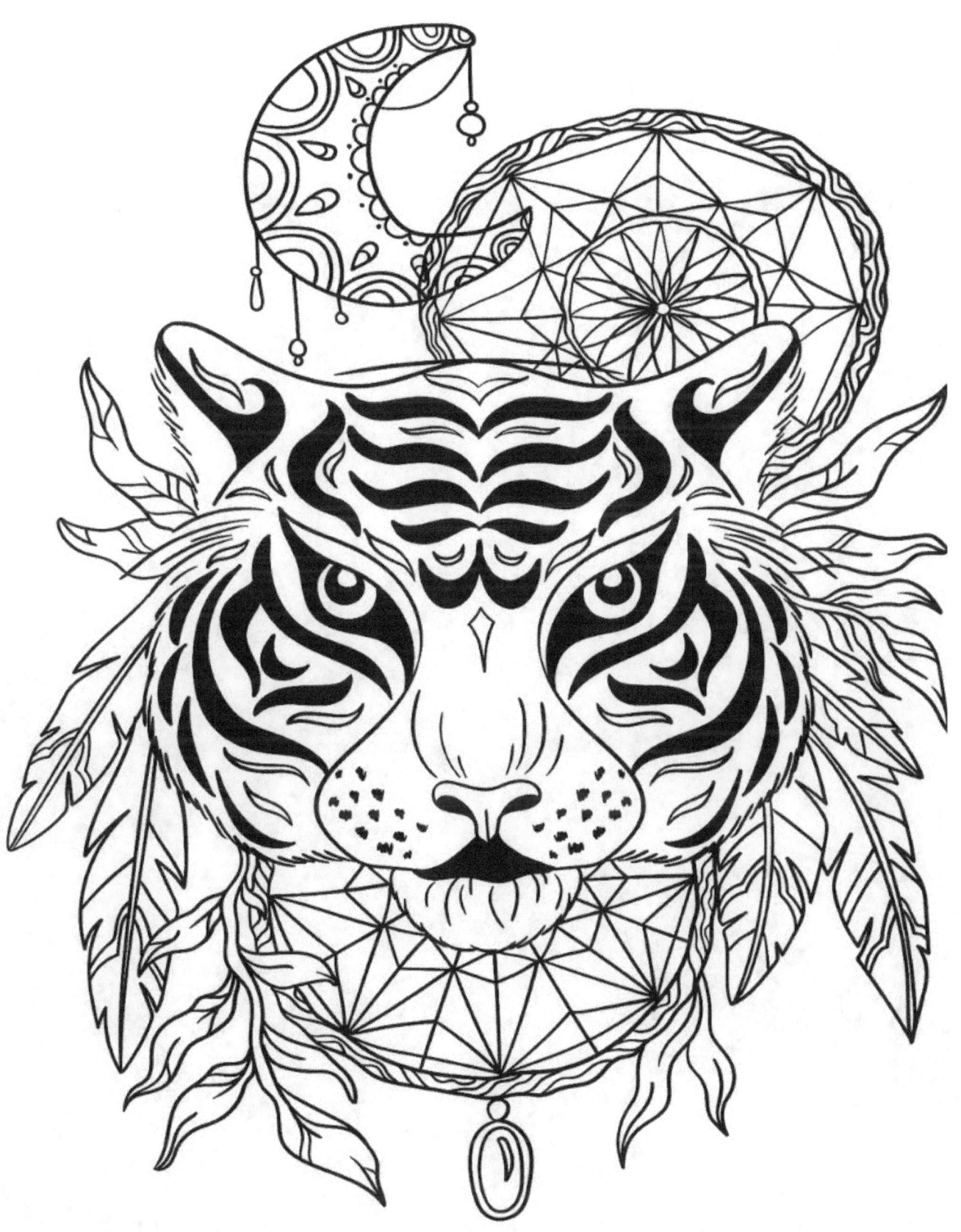

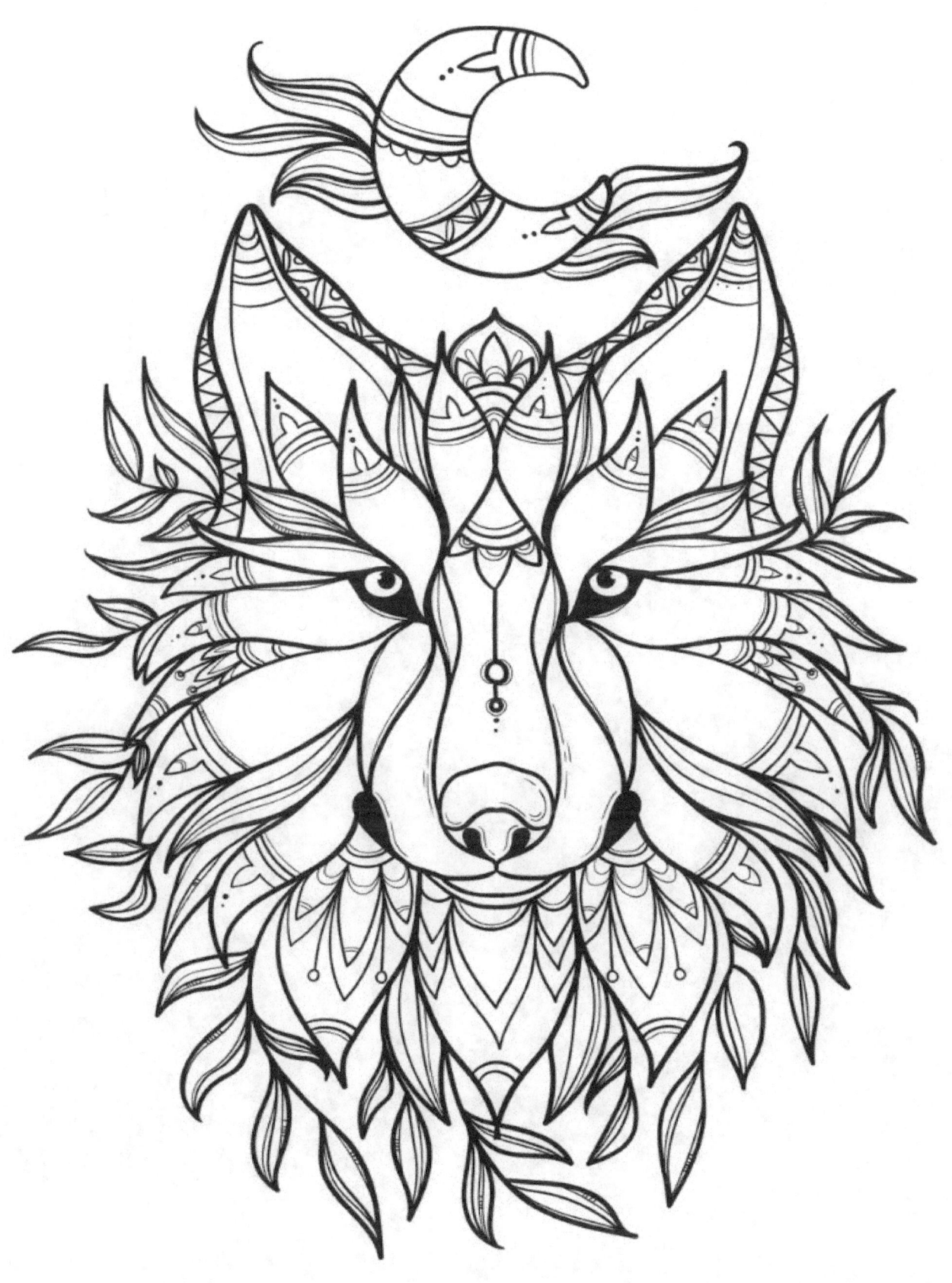

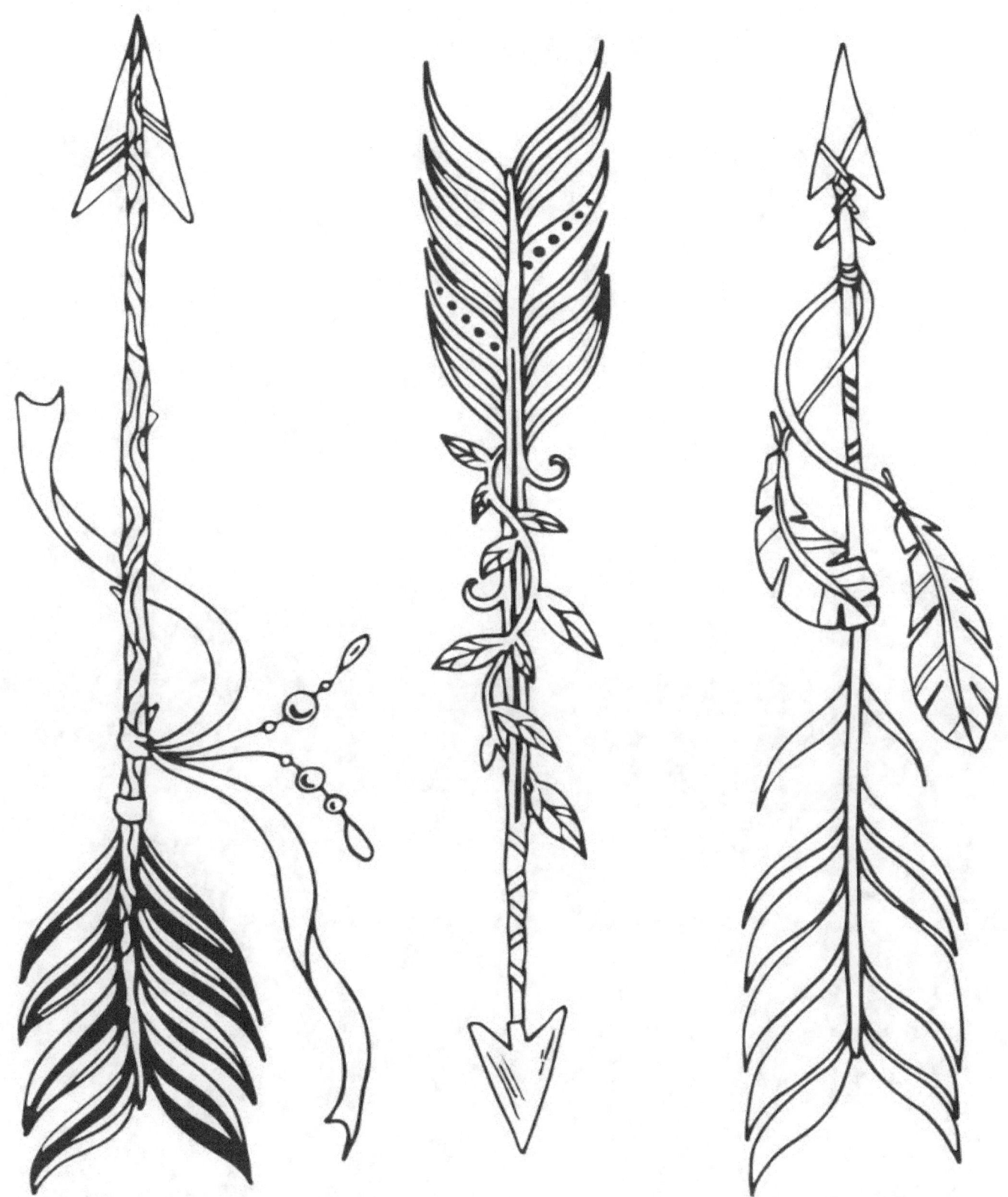

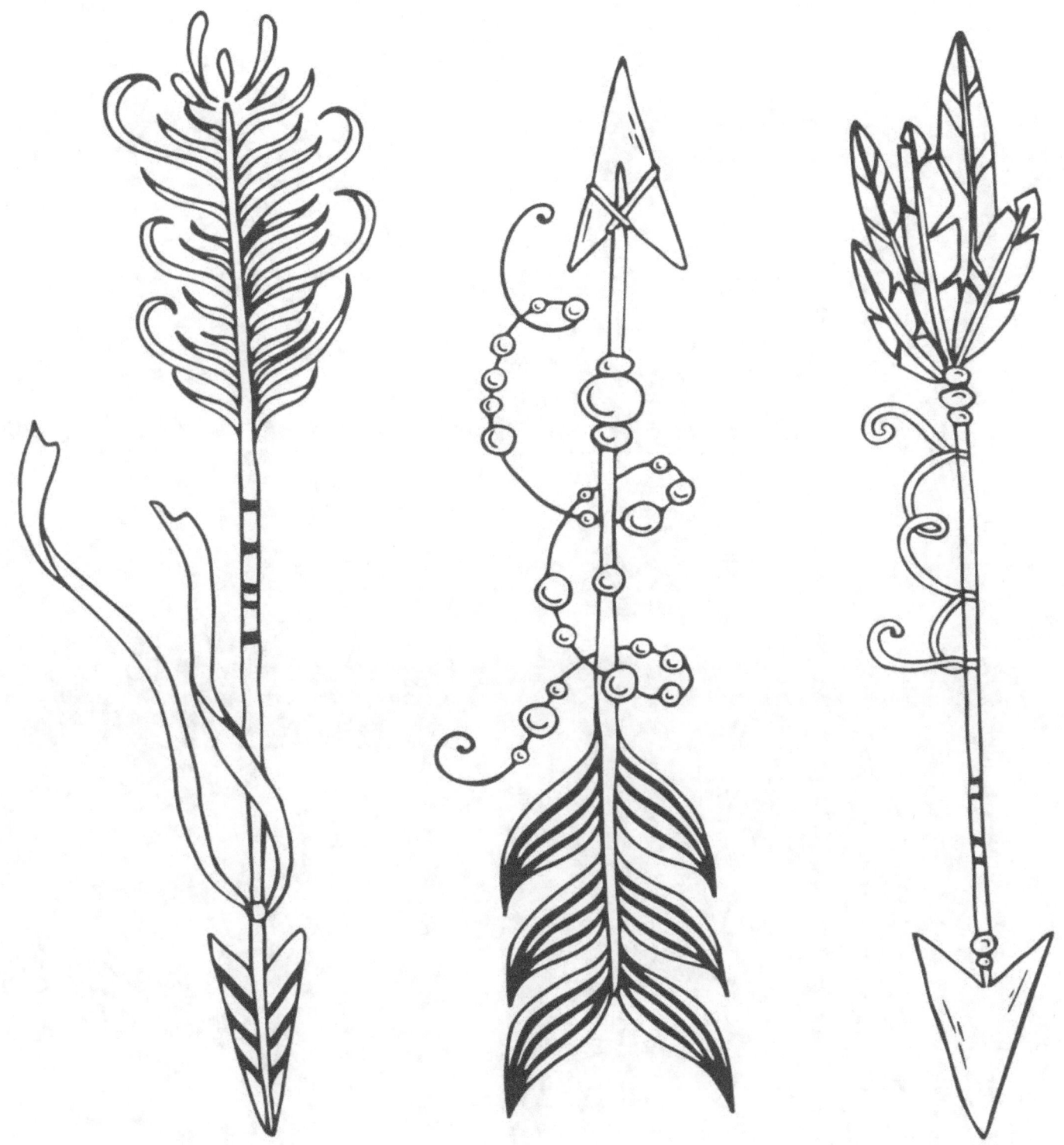

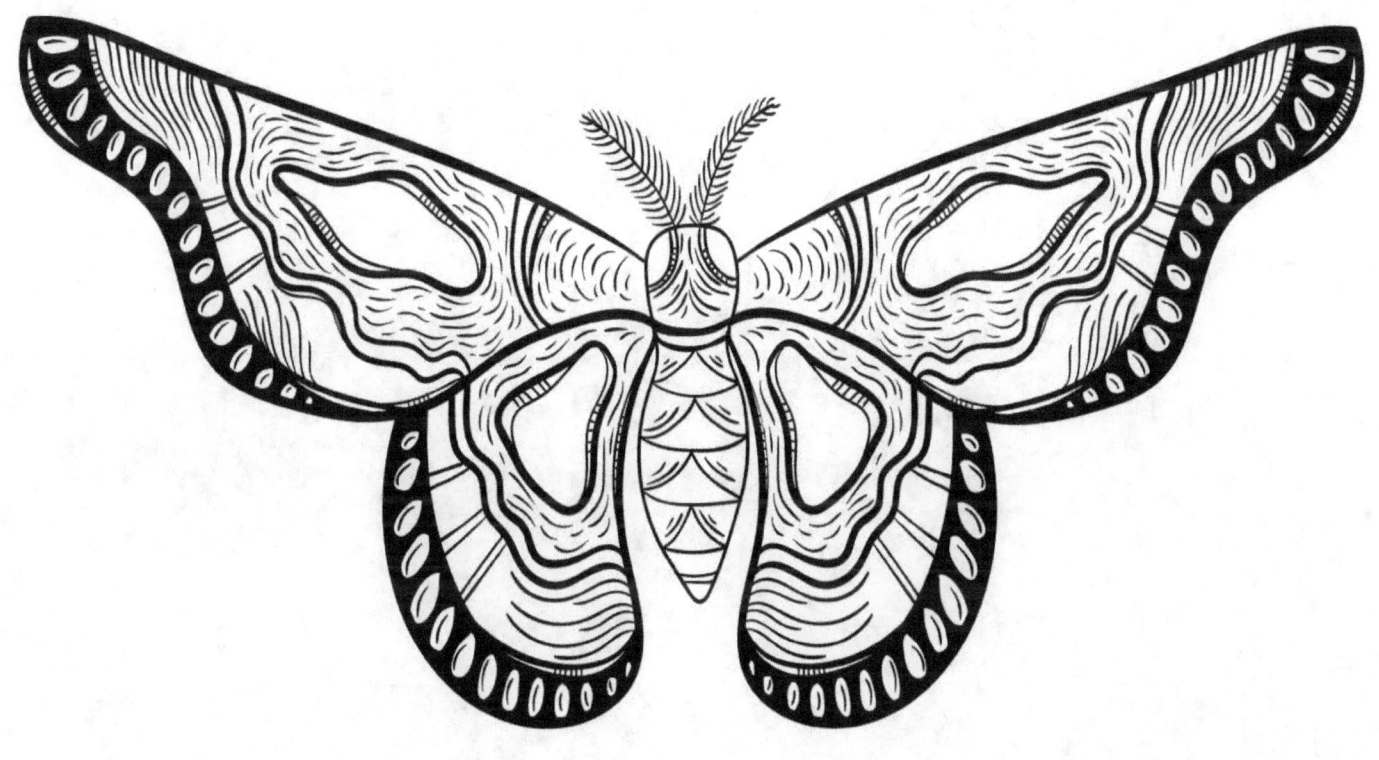

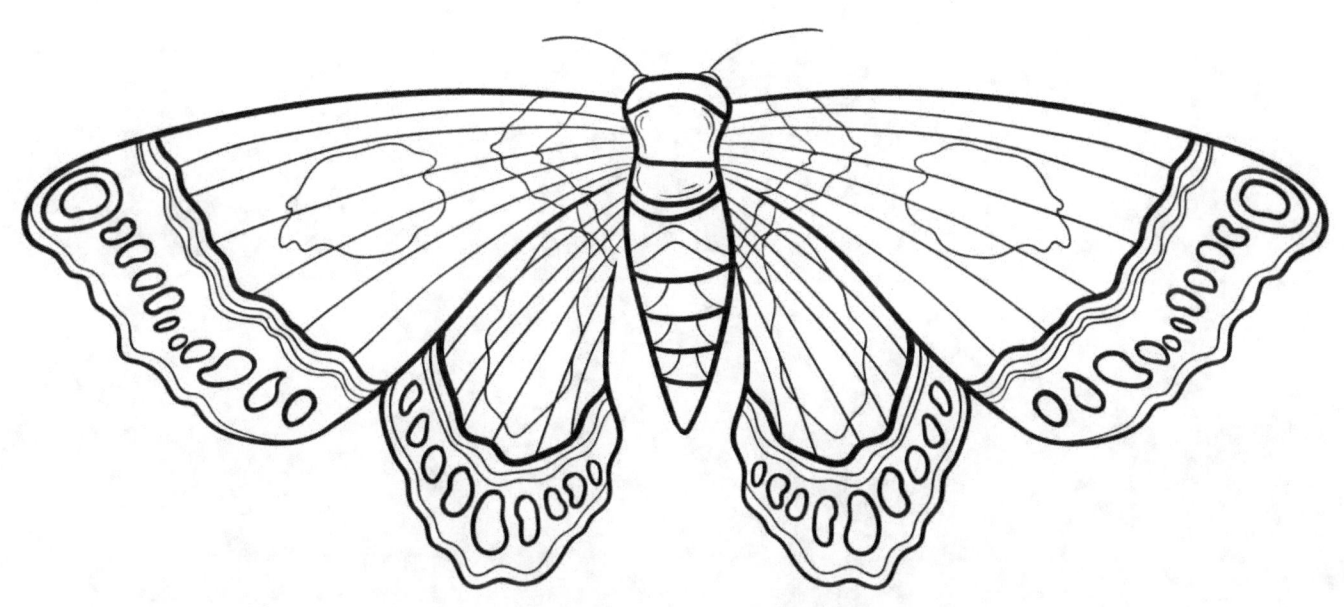

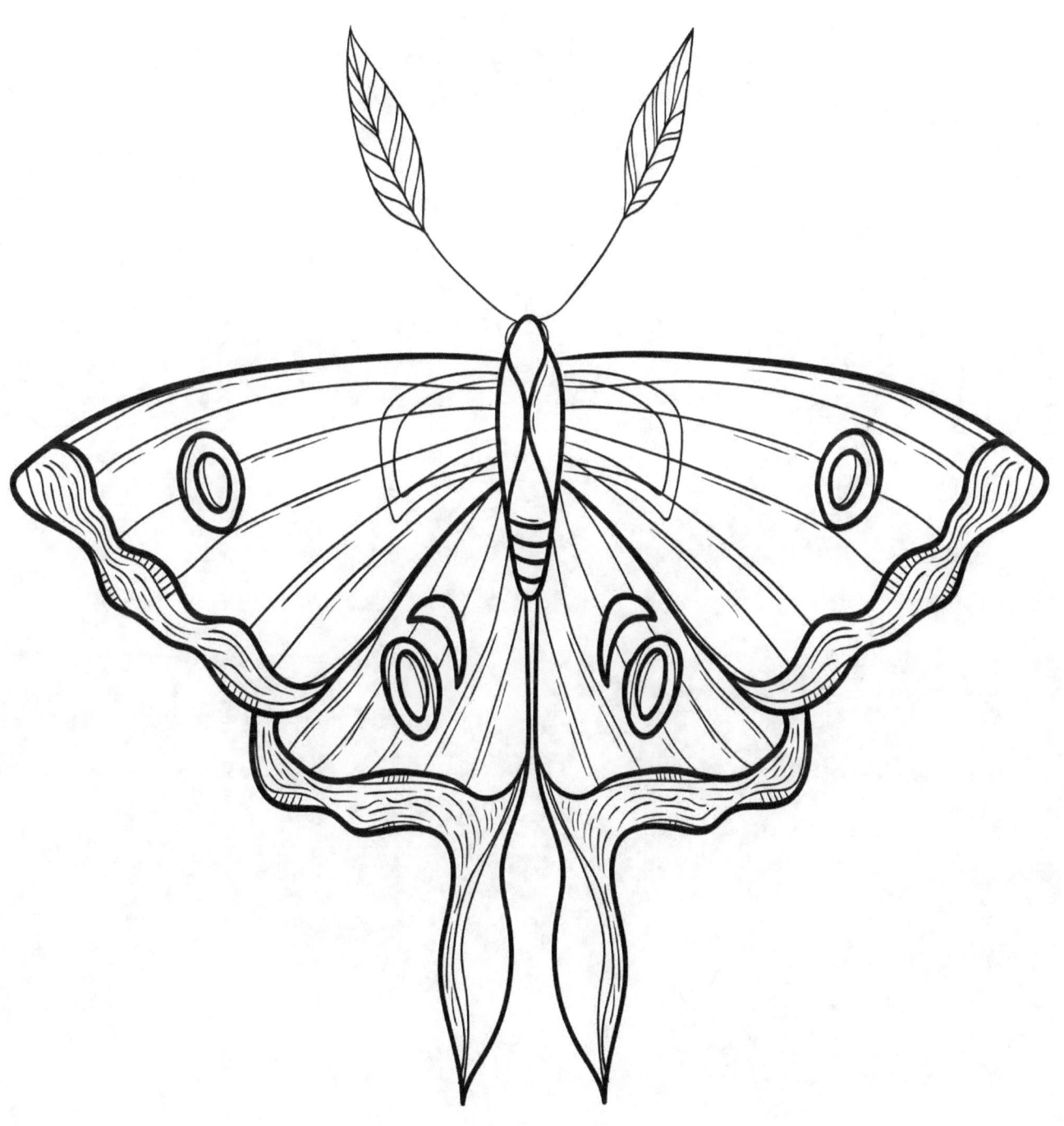

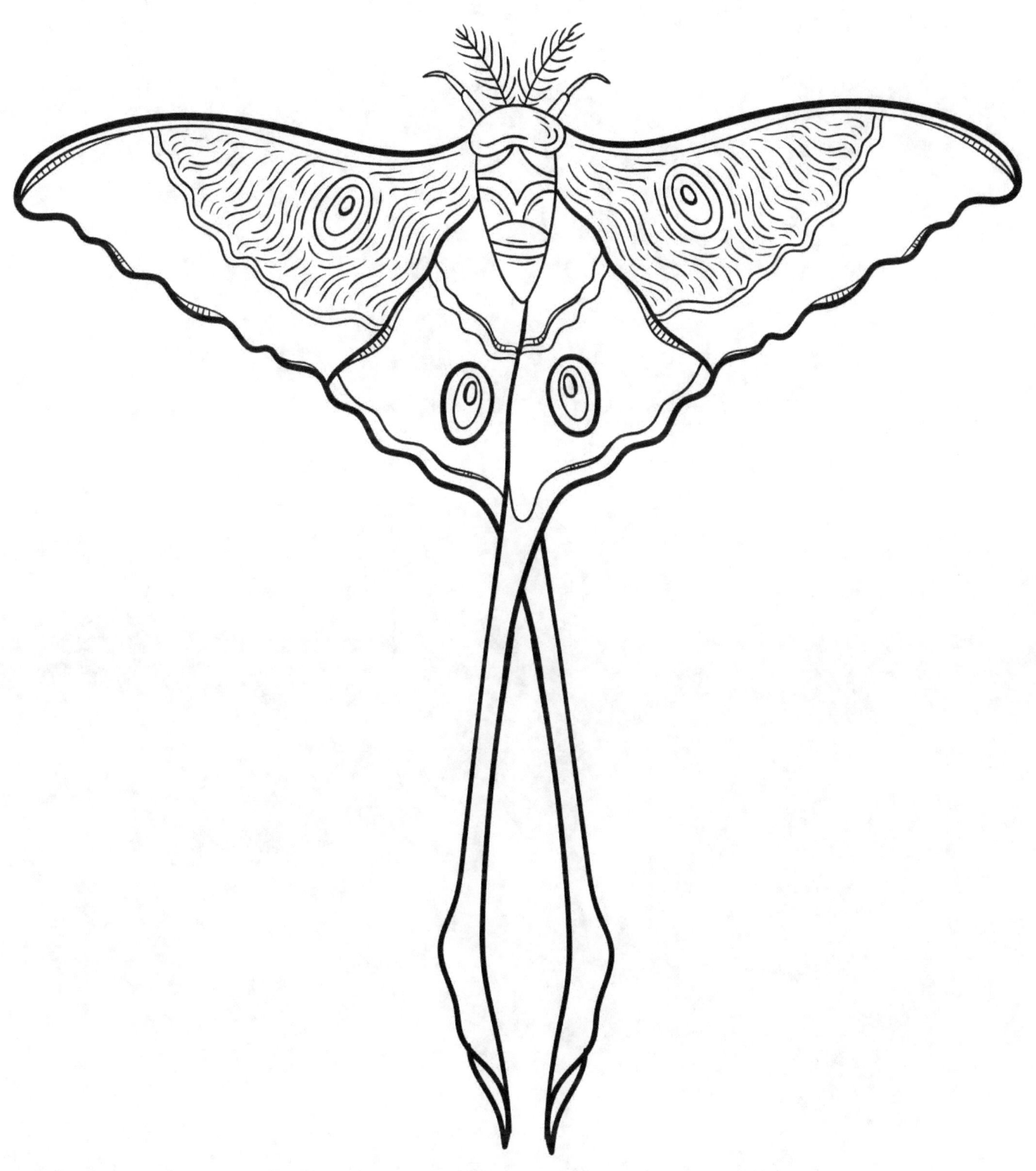

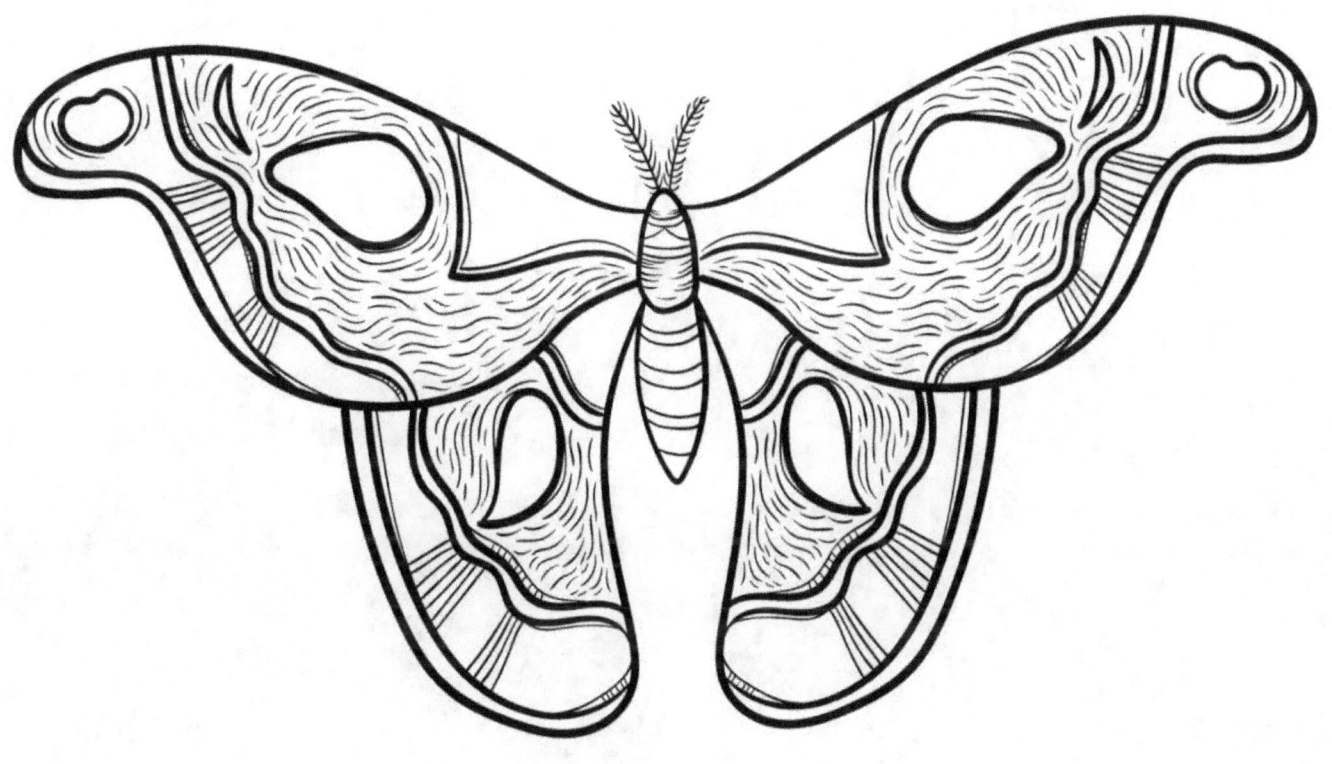

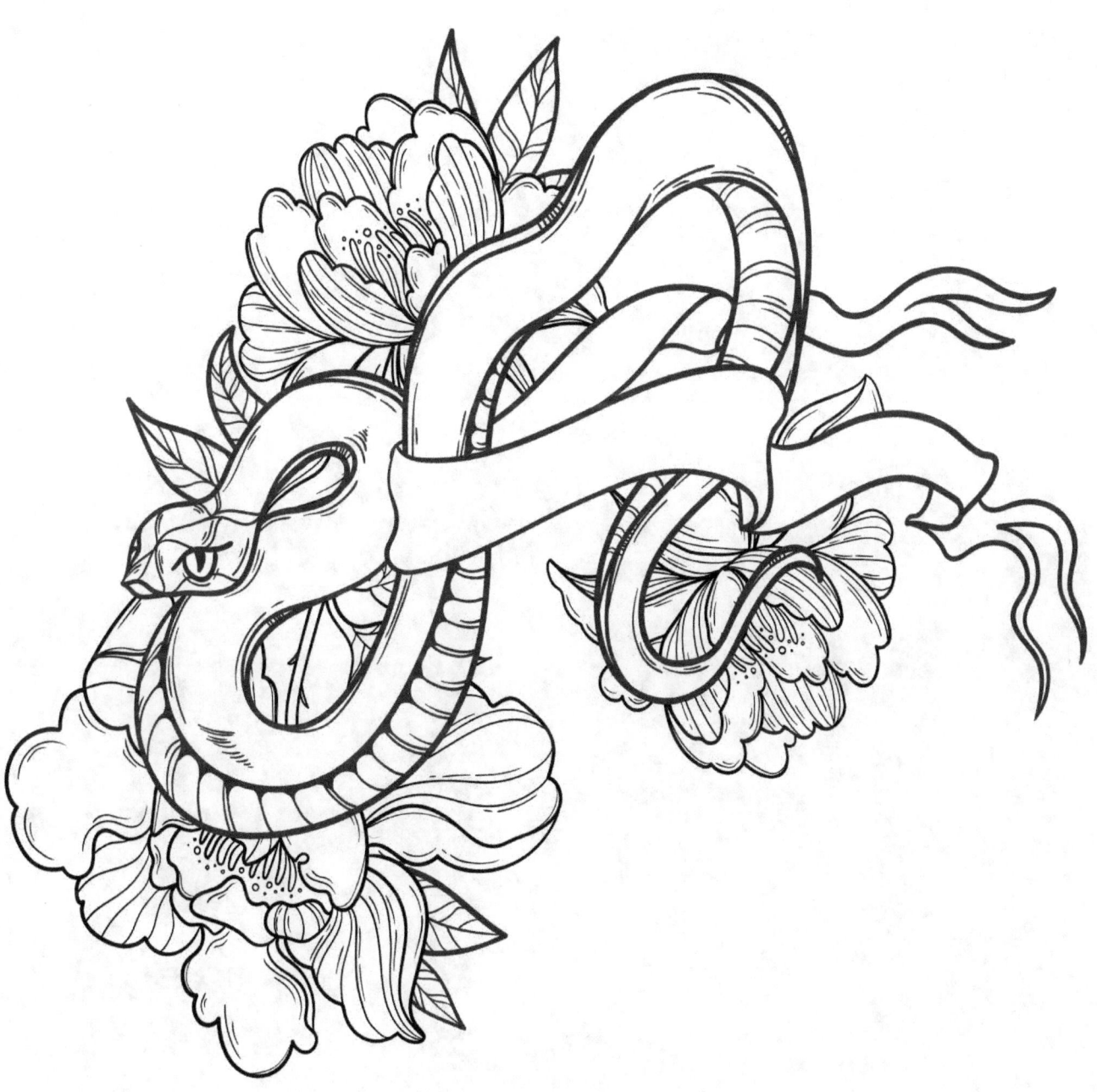

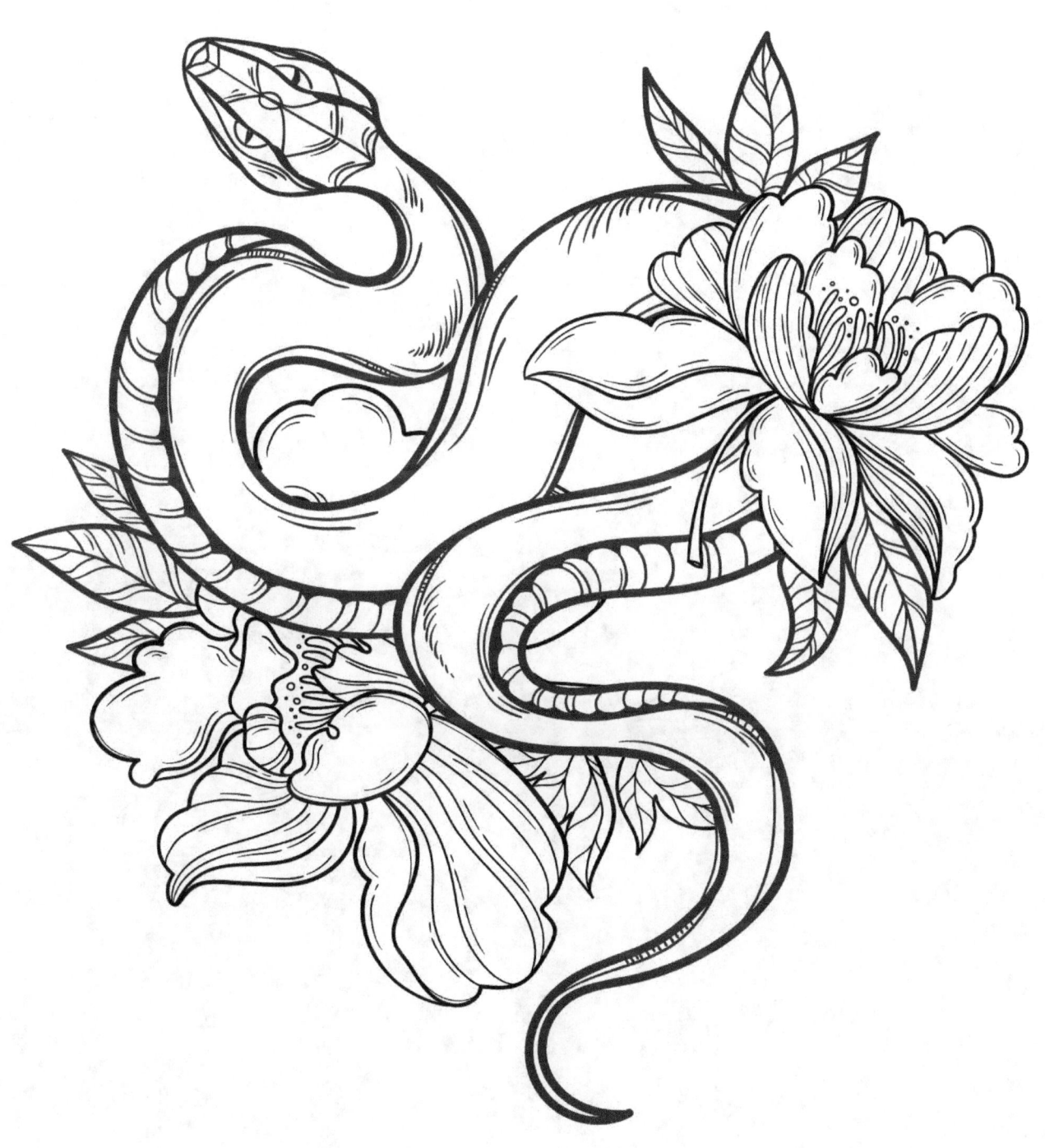

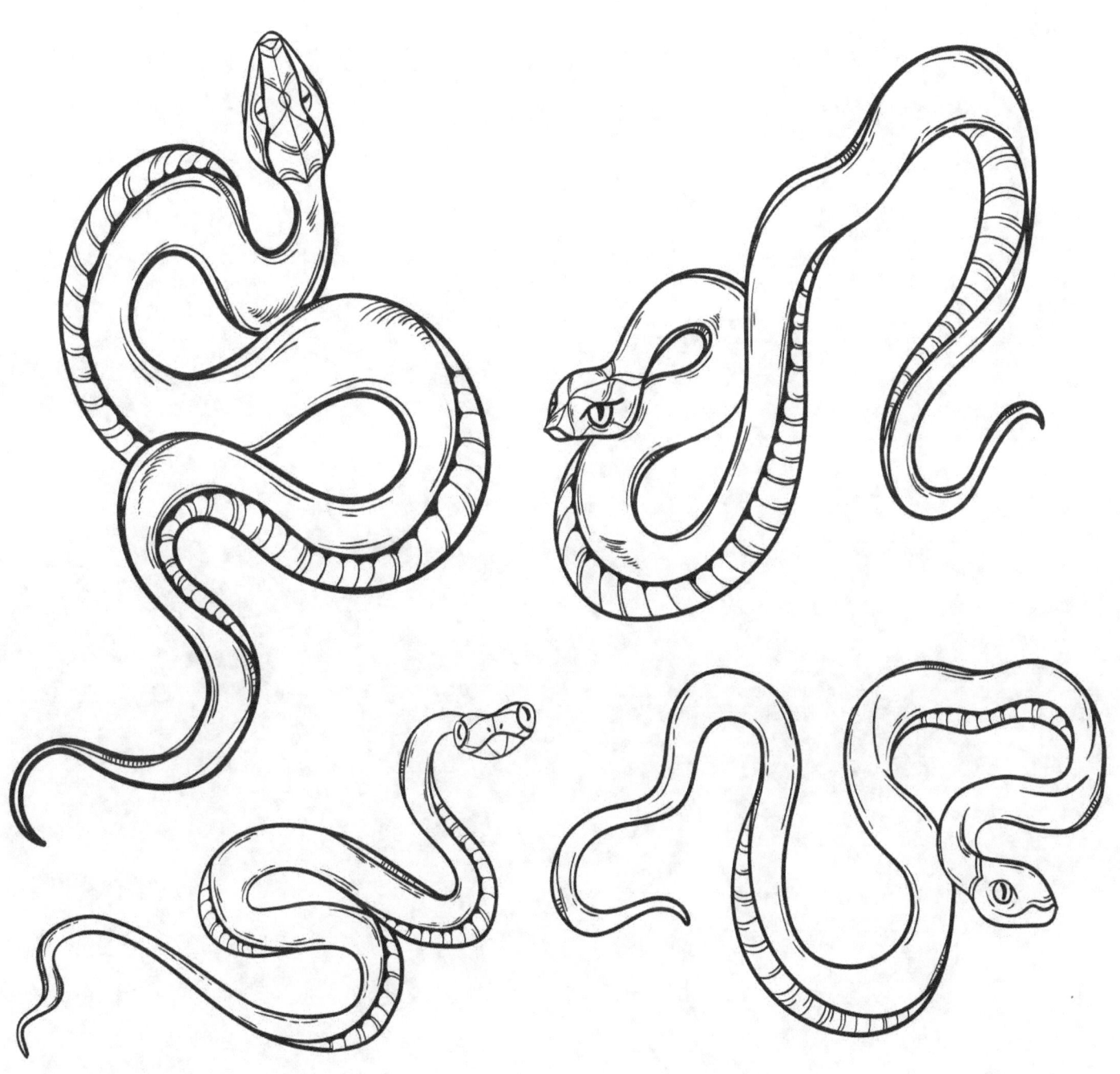

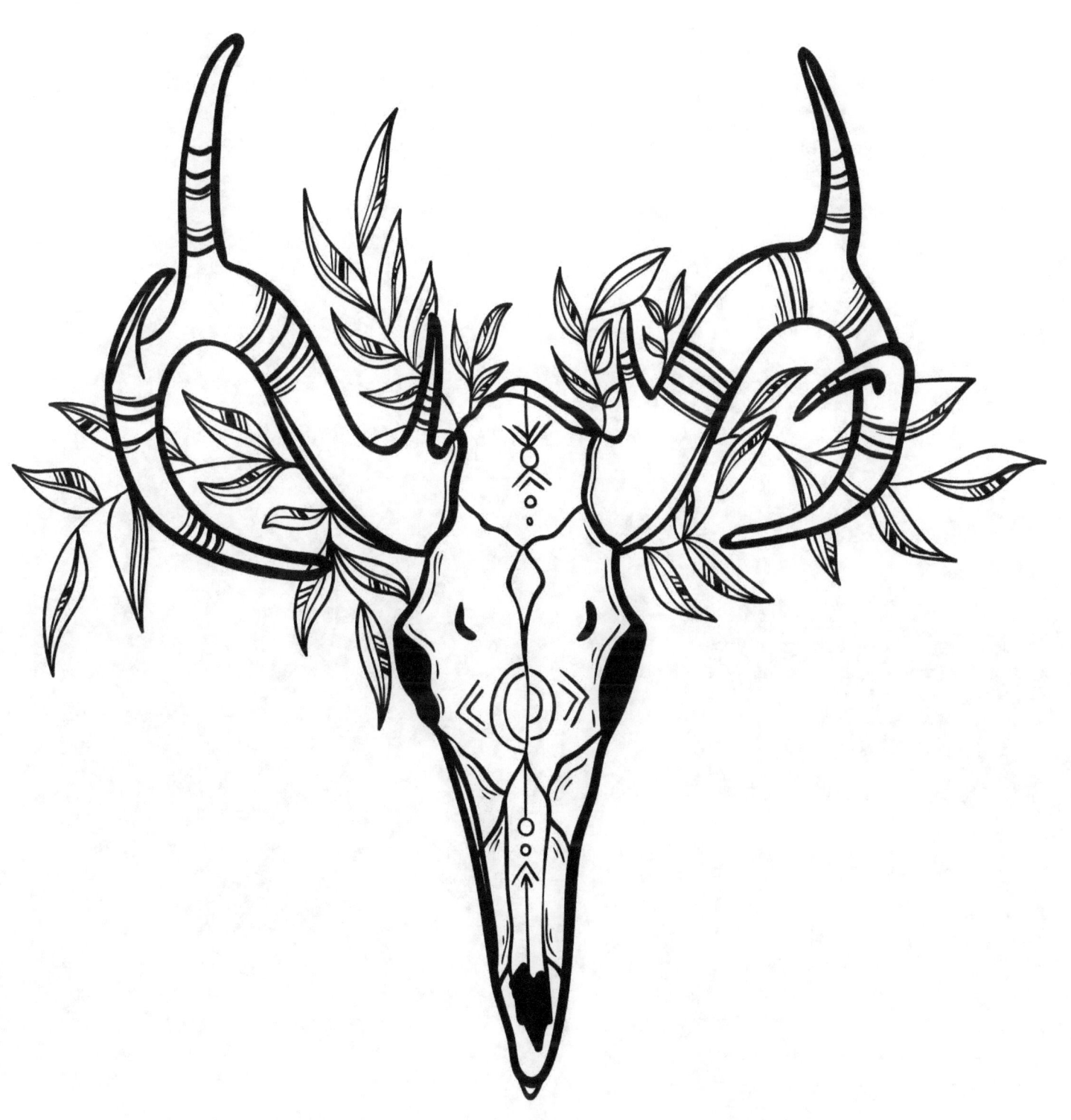

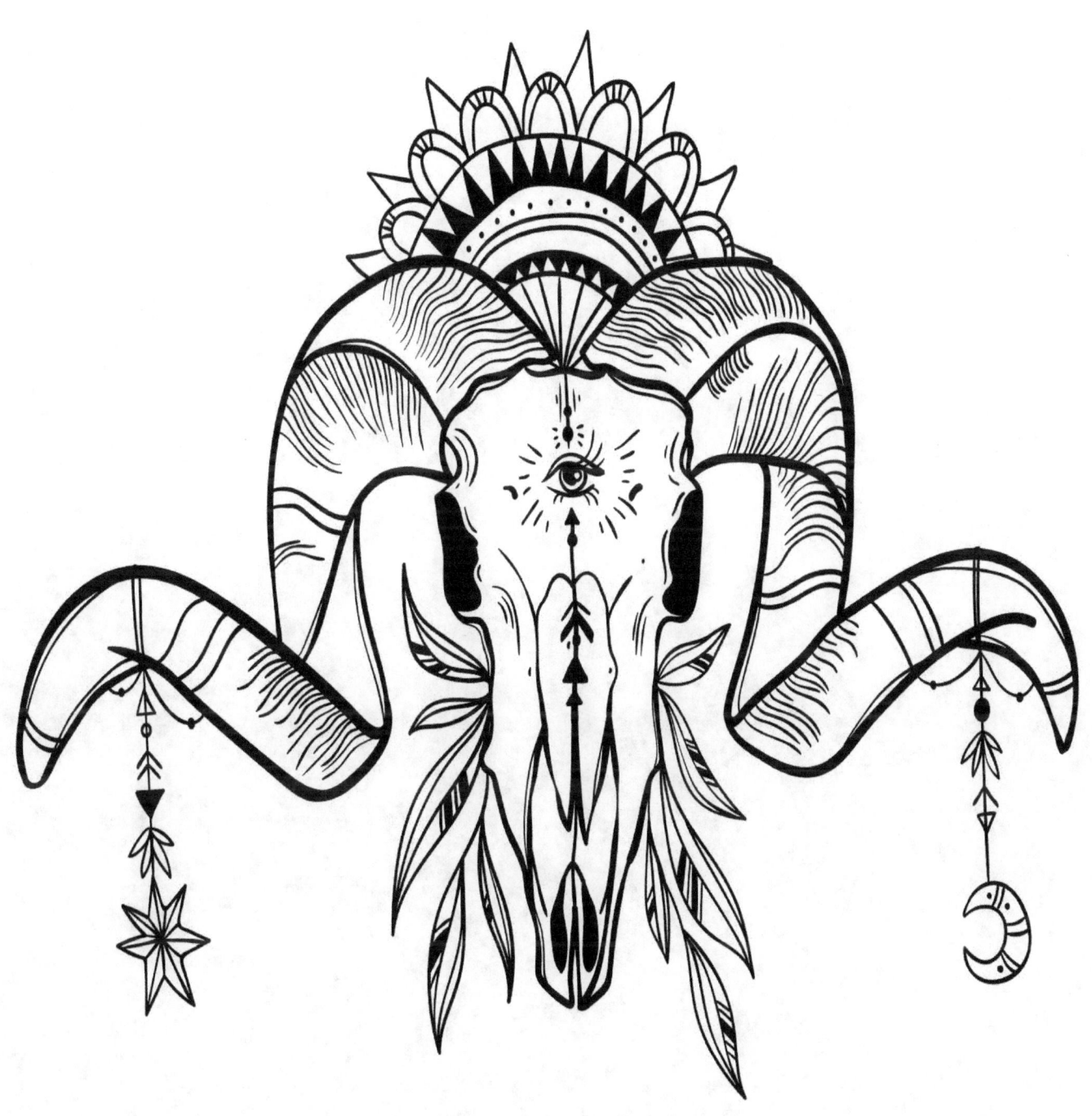

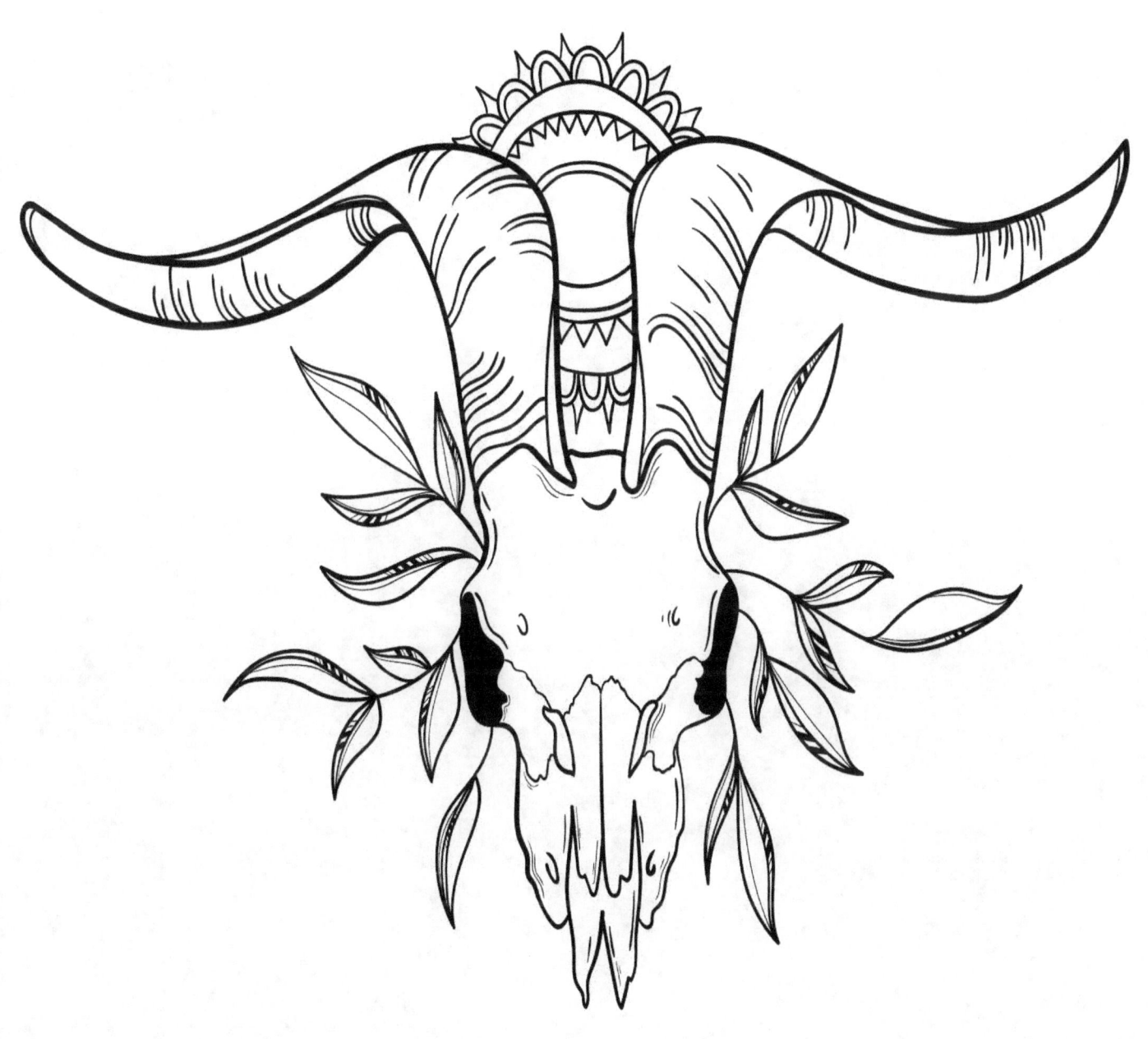

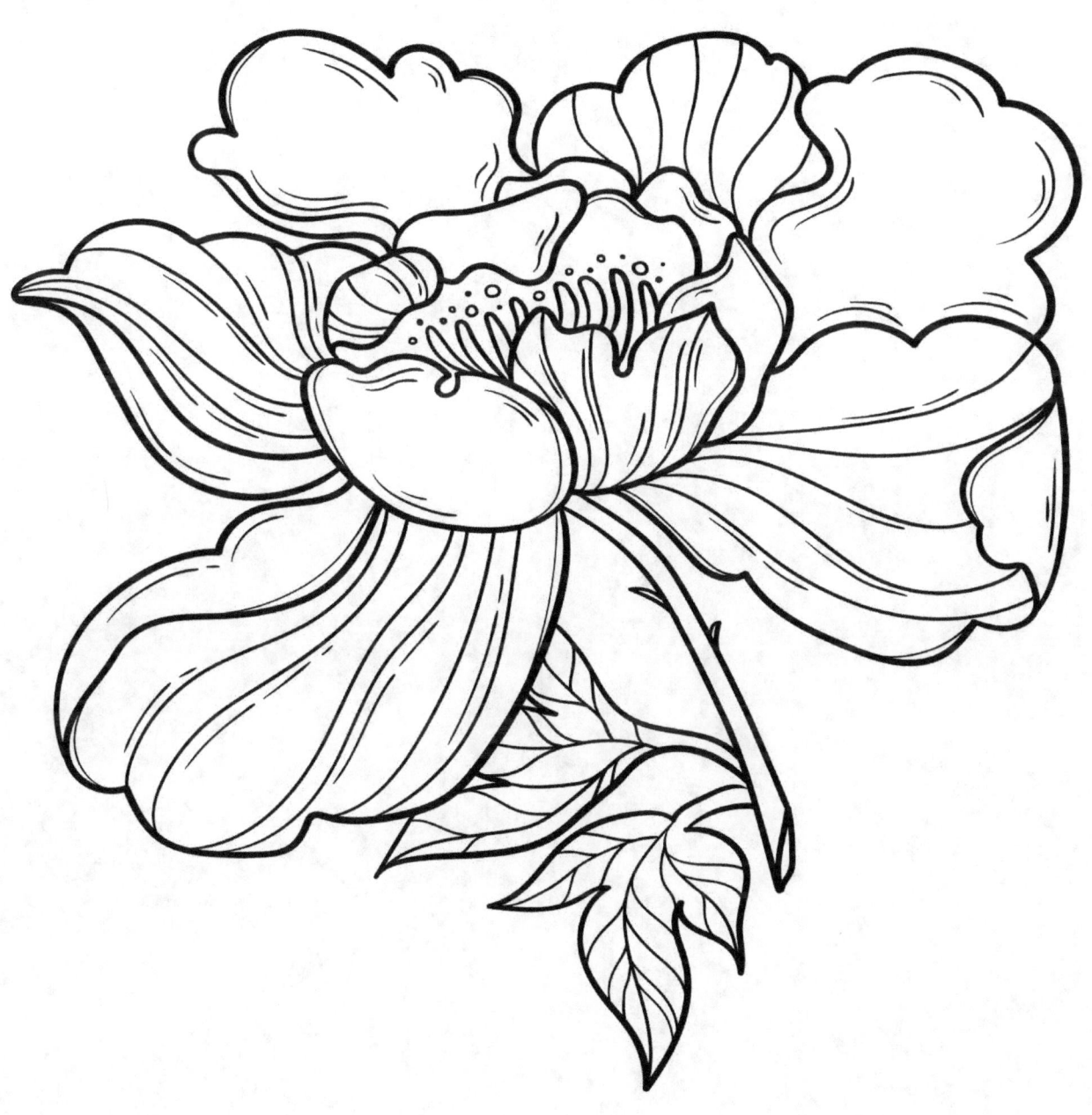

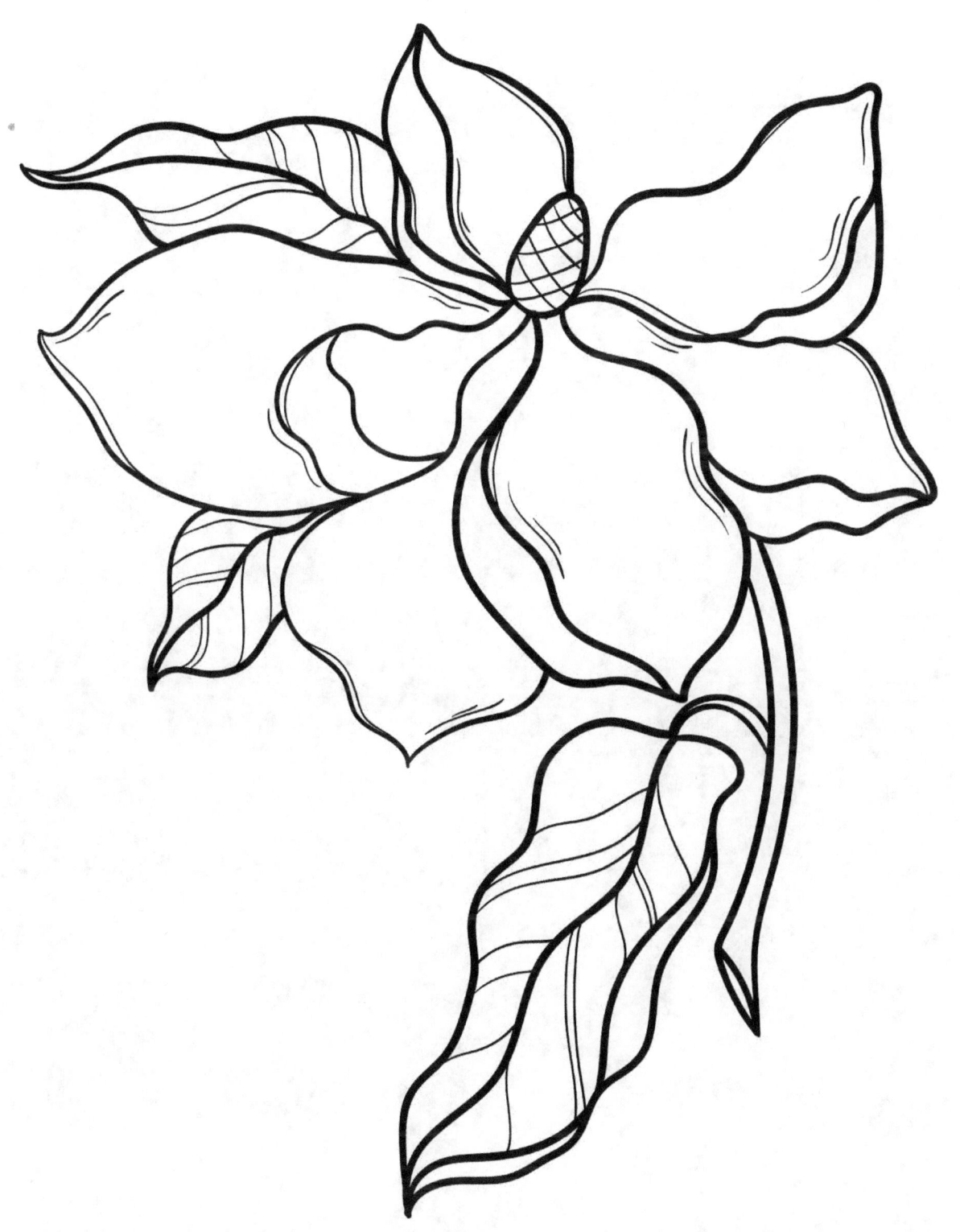

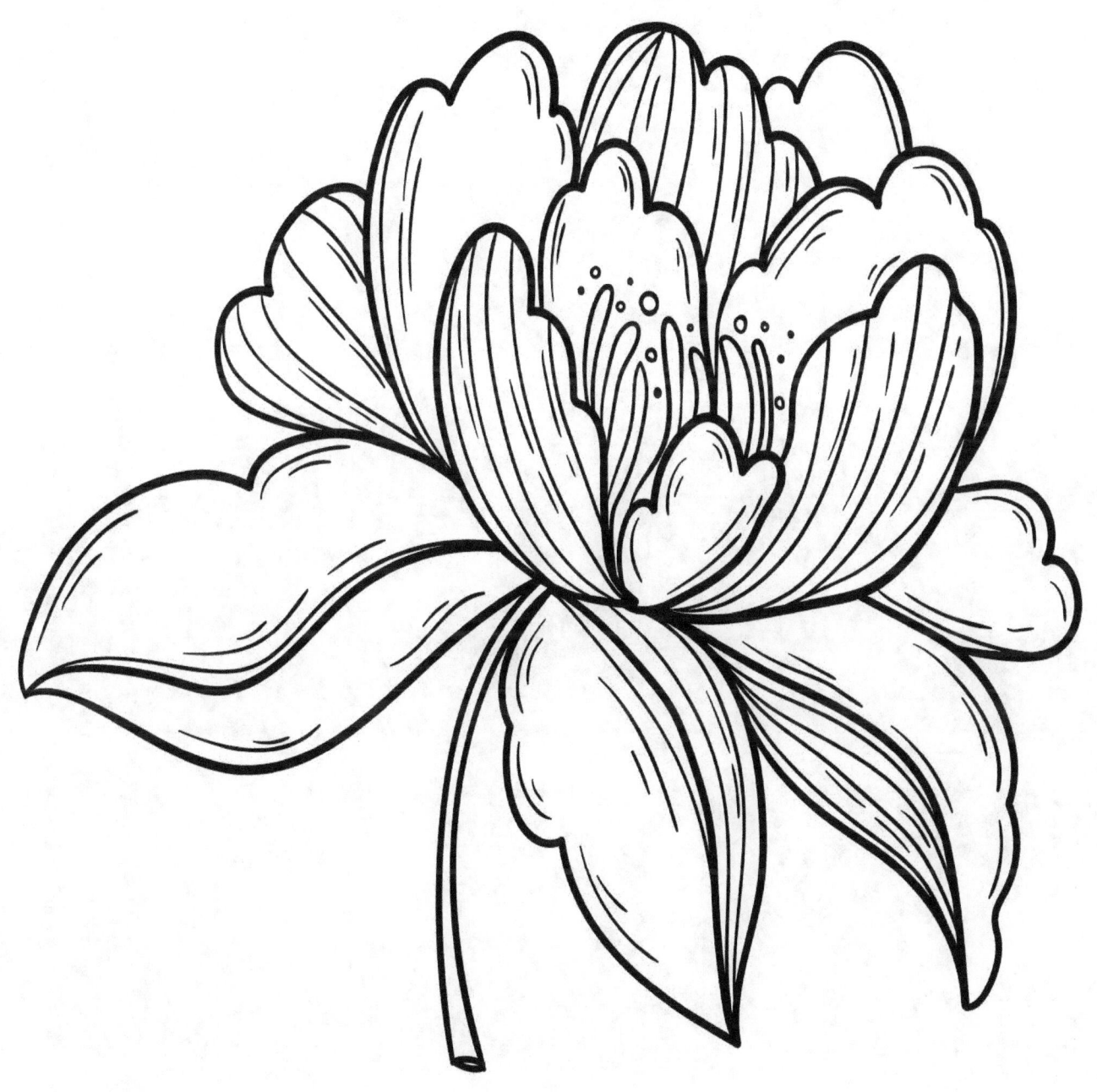

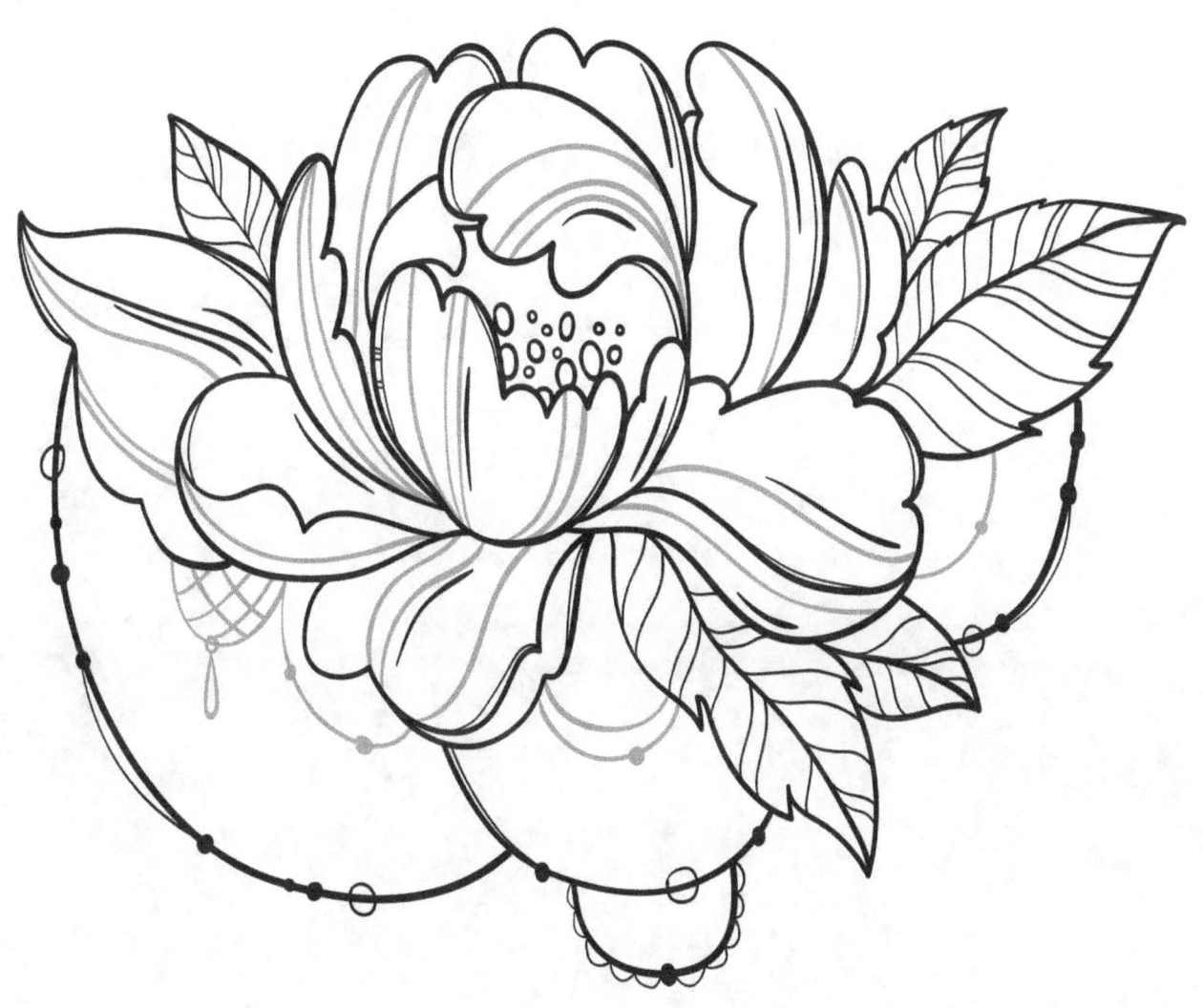

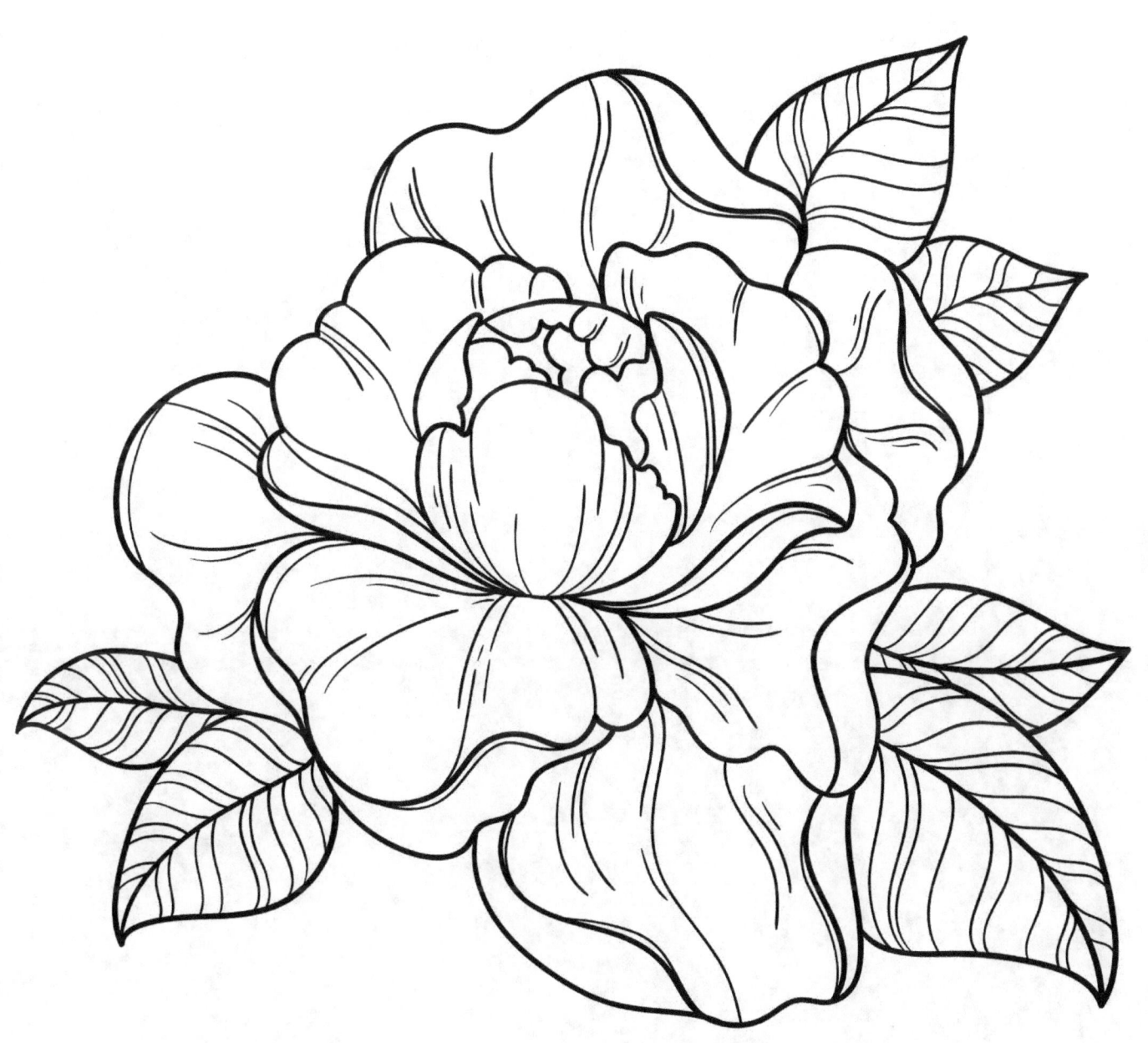

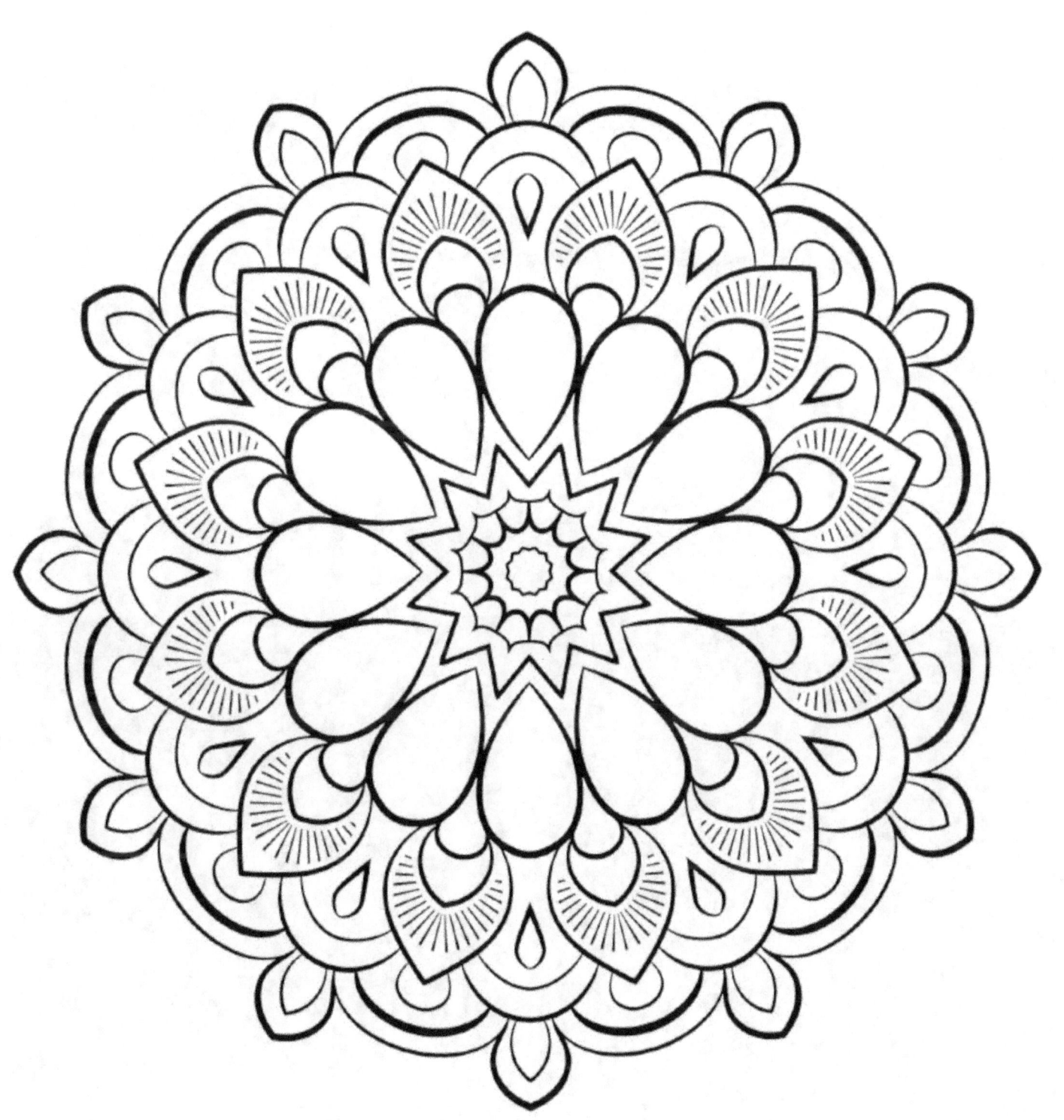

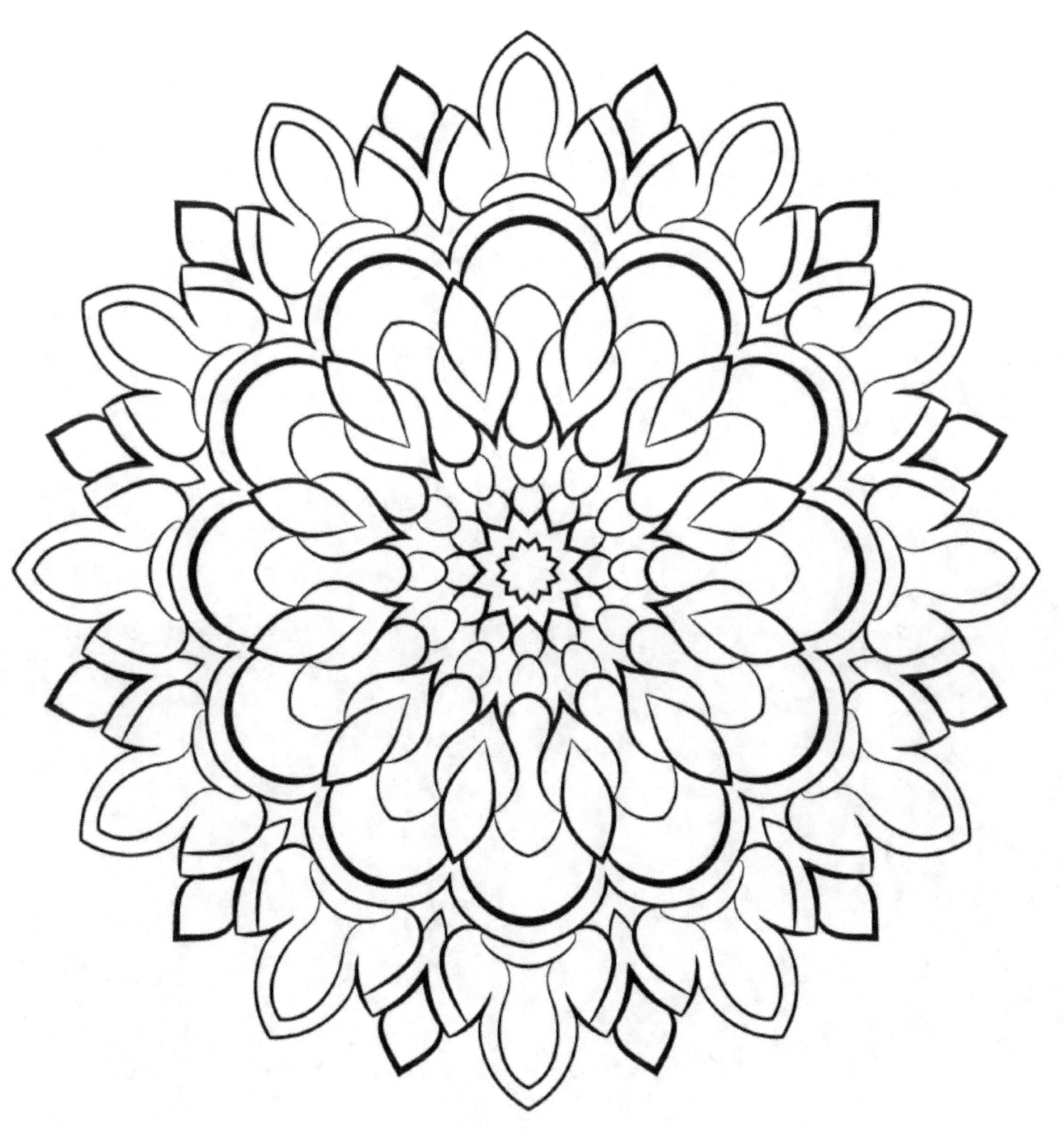

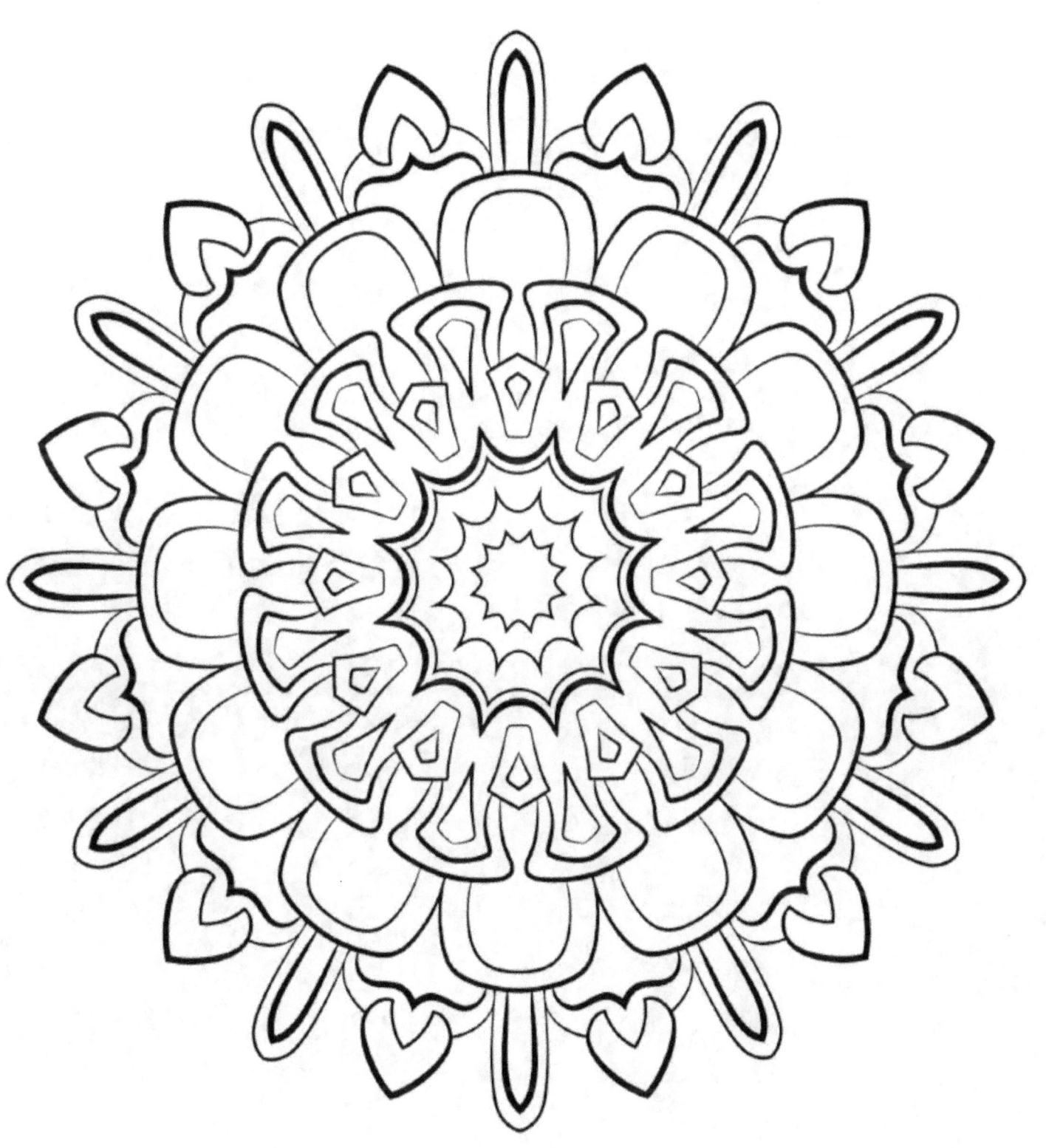

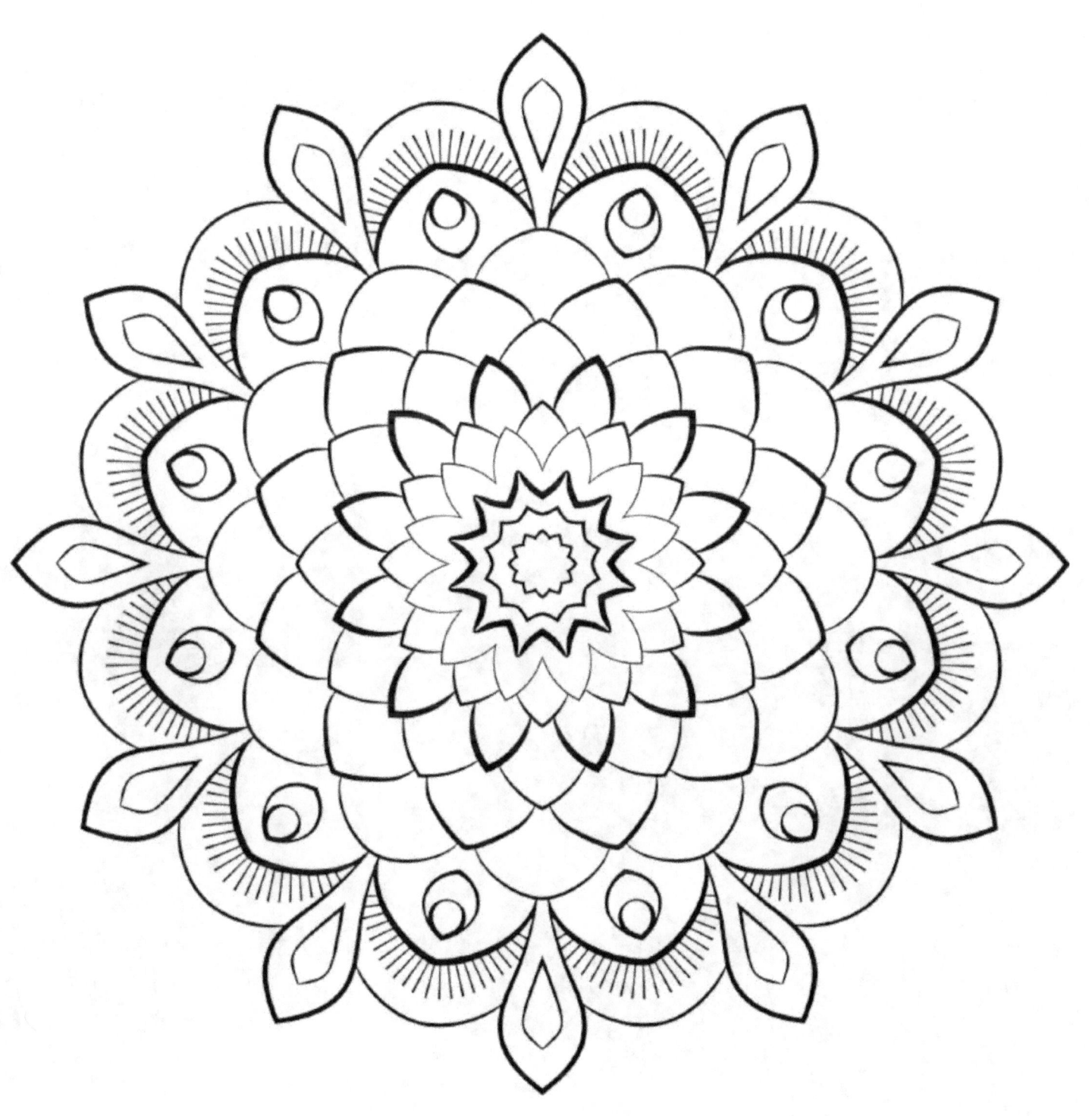

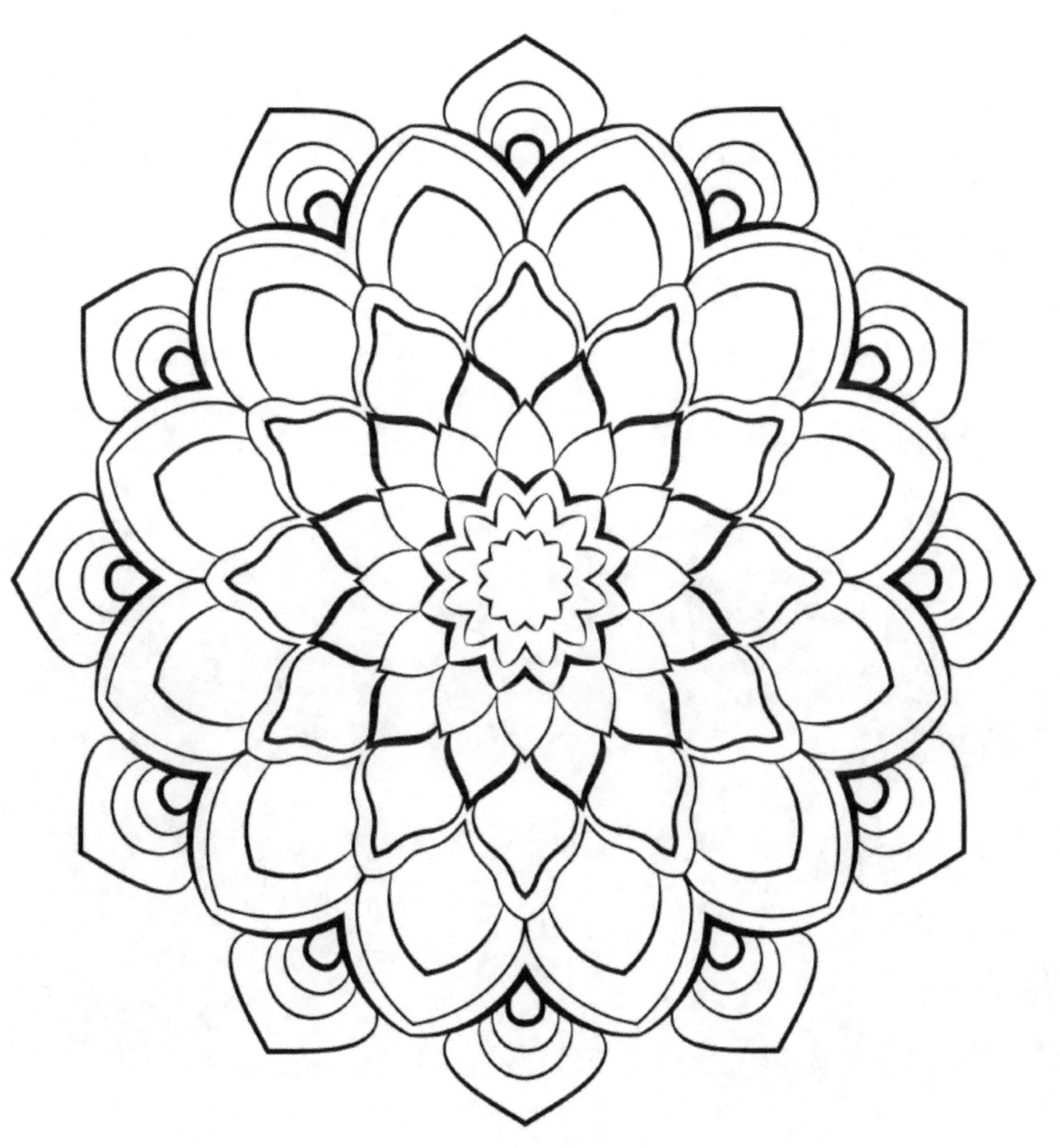

www.ingramcontent.com/pod-product-compliance
Lightning Source LLC
Chambersburg PA
CBHW080847170526
45158CB00009B/2662

* 9 7 8 1 0 8 2 0 9 0 4 4 8 *